STECK-VAUGHN

COMPREHENSION SKILLS

CONTEXT

Linda Ward Beech

Tara McCarthy

Donna Townsend

www.steck-vaughn.com

Editorial Director:	Diane Schnell
Project Editor:	Anne Souby
Associate Director of Design:	Cynthia Ellis
Design Manager:	Cynthia Hannon
Media Researcher:	Christina Berry
Production:	Rusty Kay
Cover Illustration:	Stephanie Carter
Cover Production:	Alan Klemp
Photographs:	©PhotoDisc (both)

ISBN 0-7398-2646-8

1 2 3 4 5 6 7 8 9 0 BNG 04 03 02 01 00

Using context means learning a new word by looking at the words around it. In this book you will learn new words by looking at the context.

What is context? Suppose someone asked you, "Did you get the tomatoes?" If you were in a city, you might go to the store to buy tomatoes. If you were on a farm, you might go to the garden and pick tomatoes from a vine. In the context of a city, people think of a store when they think of tomatoes. In the context of a farm, people think of a garden when they think of tomatoes.

What Is Context?

Context means all the words in a sentence or all the sentences in a paragraph. In a sentence all the words together make up the context. In a paragraph all the sentences together make up the context. You can use the context to figure out the meaning of unknown words.

Try It!

The following paragraph has a word that you may not know. See whether you can use the context (the sentences and other words in the paragraph) to find out what the word means.

> It was midnight. Mr. Blake had been driving for a long time. He began to feel **drowsy**. His eyes fluttered shut, and his head nodded forward. He awoke with a jerk a second later. "It's time for me to stop driving," he thought. Mr. Blake pulled over at the next motel.

If you don't know what **drowsy** means, you can decide by using the context. The paragraph contains these words:

Clue: his eyes fluttered shut

Clue: his head nodded forward

Clue: he awoke

Find these clues in the paragraph and circle them. What words do you think of when you read the clues? You might think of *tired*. What other words do you think of? Write the words below:

____

Did you write *sleepy*? The context clue words tell you that **drowsy** means "sleepy."

Using What You Know

Below are some paragraphs with words left out. Read the paragraphs. Look at the context. Then fill in the blanks with words about you.

I like to eat ________________ because it is so ________________ and ________________ . ________________ is my favorite food. If I could, I would eat it ________________ .

One time I traveled to ________________ . I had a wonderful time. I ________________ and ________________ . My favorite part was ________________ .

On Saturday I like to ________________ . I invite my ________________ and ________________ . They bring ________________ , and we eat ________________ .

I think the best job for me would be ________________ . I think this would be a good job because I like to ________________ and am good at ________________ .

Once I grew some ________________ . I ________________ and ________________ . It took ________________ for them to get ________________ .

Working with Context

This book asks questions that you can answer by using context clues in paragraphs. There are two kinds of paragraphs. The paragraphs in the first part of this book have blank spaces in them. You can use the context clues in the paragraphs to decide which word should go in each space. Here is an example:

Elizabeth Blackwell was the first woman doctor in the United States. She tried to get into many __1__ schools before she was finally accepted. Later she opened a hospital. It was run __2__ by women.

__B__ **1.** **A.** music **B.** medical **C.** beauty **D.** special

______ **2.** **A.** entirely **B.** darkly **C.** softly **D.** fast

Look at the answer words for blank 1. Treat the paragraph as a puzzle. Which pieces don't fit? Which piece fits best? Try putting each word in the blank. See which one makes the most sense. Doctors don't go to *music* schools or *beauty* schools. Doctors do go to a *special* school. *Special* is a possible answer. But *medical* is even better. The correct answer is *medical*, answer **B**. Now try to answer question 2 on your own.

The paragraphs in the second part of this book are different. For these you figure out the meaning of a word that is printed in **dark letters** in the paragraph. Here is an example:

Daffodils are a sign of spring. Their bright yellow color and long, thin leaves are easy to spot. Wild daffodils cover hillsides in the country. Other kinds are found in city parks.

The word in dark type is **daffodils**. Find the context clues. Then find the answer words that mean the same as **daffodils**.

______ **3.** In this paragraph, the word **daffodils** means

A. a kind of bird **C.** a kind of animal

B. a kind of flower **D.** a kind of kite

To check your answers, turn to page 60.

How to Use This Book

This book has 25 units. In units 1 through 12, you will read stories with blank spaces where words have been left out. Use the context of each story to help you choose words to fill the blanks. In units 13 through 25, the stories have words printed in dark letters. Use the context of each story to help you choose the correct meaning for the word in dark letters.

You can check your answers by looking at pages 61 and 62. Write the number of correct answers in the score box at the top of the page.

Hints

- Look for context clues while you are reading the stories. Ask yourself, Where is this story happening? Who is in the story? What is the story about?
- Look at each answer word carefully. Put each answer word in the paragraph. The paragraph is like a puzzle. Which words don't fit? Which one fits best?
- If you can't find the answer the first time, look back at the story. Then try the answer words again.

Challenge

Try this special challenge. Read each story. Choose the correct answer word. Then try to write sentences of your own, using the correct answer words.

Writing

On pages 30–31 and 58–59, there are paragraphs for you to complete. Write a word or sentence that makes sense in each paragraph. You will find suggested answers on page 60, but your answers may be very different.

Most auroras appear high in the far northern and southern night skies. They are ___1___ streaks of colored lights. Green is the most ___2___ color, but red and purple are often seen.

_____ 1. A. anxious B. spectacular C. low D. painted

_____ 2. A. common B. even C. difficult D. unlikely

Computers are fun and ___3___ machines. They help us store and work with information. Some people use them to ___4___ math problems. Others like them just for playing games.

_____ 3. A. lazy B. helpless C. useful D. awkward

_____ 4. A. earn B. solve C. refuse D. destroy

The cheetah is a big cat. It is known for its great speed as it runs short ___5___. It uses its sleek body and long, powerful legs to run fast. This cat's claws help it grab the ground as it races to catch its ___6___.

_____ 5. A. days B. evenings C. naps D. stretches

_____ 6. A. bath B. water C. quarry D. apple

Fossils are the traces or remains of living things from millions of years ago. They include shells, bones, and teeth that have been ___7___ in rocks. Petrified wood and dinosaur tracks are also fossil ___8___.

_____ 7. A. retained B. grown C. sold D. thrown

_____ 8. A. rows B. specimens C. echoes D. names

SCORE

In 1770 many people in Boston, Massachusetts, were angry. They did not like the new laws England had passed for them. Crispus Attucks thought they should ___9___. He led a group of ___10___ citizens through the town. The British troops fired shots at the crowd. Crispus was the first to be killed. This African American man, who had once been a slave, became a hero.

______ **9.** **A.** declare **B.** look **C.** arrive **D.** protest

______ **10.** **A.** curious **B.** warm **C.** enraged **D.** silly

---

Denmark is a country in Europe. It owns a large island that is far away from Europe. This island is ___11___ in the Atlantic Ocean. It is so far north that most of it is covered by an ice cap. This island is ___12___ Greenland.

______ **11.** **A.** hanging **B.** situated **C.** safe **D.** blocked

______ **12.** **A.** named **B.** moved **C.** lost **D.** given

---

Lightning is usually seen as a streak across the sky. Lightning in the shape of a ___13___ is called ball lightning. It is rarely seen, and no one can ___14___ why it occurs.

______ **13.** **A.** sphere **B.** square **C.** heart **D.** line

______ **14.** **A.** deny **B.** recall **C.** explain **D.** cure

---

In Scotland there is a lake called Loch Ness. Many people say they have seen a sea monster in this lake. The stories about the Loch Ness monster have made it quite ___15___. Yet there is not enough ___16___ to show that it really does exist.

______ **15.** **A.** happy **B.** famous **C.** patient **D.** old

______ **16.** **A.** time **B.** interest **C.** water **D.** proof

Bessie Coleman wanted to be a pilot. She went to France and learned how to fly. She became the first African American woman ___1___. In 1926 she was killed while she ___2___ in an air show.

______ **1.** **A.** star **B.** judge **C.** aviator **D.** doctor

______ **2.** **A.** met **B.** performed **C.** quit **D.** behaved

---

A telescope is used to make ___3___ stars look closer and larger. It looks like a long tube. The light from a star enters one end of the tube. Two mirrors are used to ___4___ the light to an eyepiece. When you look through the eyepiece, you are able to get a better view of the star.

______ **3.** **A.** remote **B.** narrow **C.** late **D.** wild

______ **4.** **A.** attach **B.** brush **C.** tow **D.** reflect

---

The ostrich is the largest bird in the world. It can grow to a height of eight feet and can weigh three hundred ___5___. The ostrich can't fly, but it can run fast to ___6___ from danger.

______ **5.** **A.** pounds **B.** miles **C.** bikes **D.** insects

______ **6.** **A.** remove **B.** escape **C.** walk **D.** block

---

Years ago the first French trappers and explorers came to South Dakota. They found the ___7___ had many tall peaks, steep ridges, and deep gullies. This land was ___8___ to cross. The French called it the Badlands. Now people like the unique beauty of the Badlands.

______ **7.** **A.** life **B.** meadow **C.** river **D.** area

______ **8.** **A.** easy **B.** lovely **C.** hazardous **D.** shallow

SCORE

The tiger lives in parts of Asia. It is the largest ___9___ of the cat family. Its fur is brownish orange with black stripes. The tiger ___10___ the woods alone as it hunts for large prey to eat.

______ **9.** **A.** food **B.** member **C.** country **D.** enemy

______ **10.** **A.** prowls **B.** eats **C.** obeys **D.** sleeps

---

Most of us can see many ___11___ of color. However, some people are colorblind. These people have a hard time telling certain colors ___12___. A few colorblind people can't see any colors at all.

______ **11.** **A.** leaves **B.** shades **C.** feet **D.** drops

______ **12.** **A.** apart **B.** below **C.** out **D.** gladly

---

The abacus is a counting ___13___. It was invented thousands of years ago. It has beads strung on wires that are attached to a frame. The beads are used to represent numbers. Math problems are ___14___ by moving the beads.

______ **13.** **A.** time **B.** force **C.** value **D.** machine

______ **14.** **A.** failed **B.** calculated **C.** avoided **D.** melted

---

The pitcher plant has a special kind of leaf. Part of each leaf bends outward and has a sweet smell that ___15___ insects. Once insects land on a leaf, they can't escape. The slippery surface makes them slide down the tube-like leaf. The insects drown in the ___16___ found at the bottom of the leaf. After a while the plant digests the insects.

______ **15.** **A.** hatches **B.** eats **C.** attracts **D.** destroys

______ **16.** **A.** joy **B.** noise **C.** desert **D.** liquid

UNIT 3

The castle was once a very important place, and it had many uses. It was a palace for the rulers of the region. Lawbreakers were held in a ___1___ that was part of the castle. The castle also served as a ___2___ for protection against enemies.

______ **1.** **A.** tree **B.** prison **C.** closet **D.** window

______ **2.** **A.** fort **B.** curtain **C.** ranch **D.** harvest

---

At a ___3___ you will see the water level rise and fall twice each day. The tides change like this because the moon and the sun pull on the earth. This pull is known as gravity. It forces the surface of the sea to pull up ___4___ toward the moon or the sun.

______ **3.** **A.** shoreline **B.** fair **C.** debate **D.** theater

______ **4.** **A.** poorly **B.** timely **C.** freshly **D.** slightly

---

Although a koala looks similar to a bear, in ___5___ it is not a bear at all. This cute, cuddly ___6___ is a marsupial. This means a mother koala will carry her baby in a pouch as it grows.

______ **5.** **A.** object **B.** fact **C.** arm **D.** hunger

______ **6.** **A.** bear **B.** insect **C.** creature **D.** savage

---

Stonehenge is a circle of huge stones. It stands on a flat ___7___ in England. It was ___8___ more than four thousand years ago. It may have been used for measuring time. But there are still many questions about how and why it was built.

______ **7.** **A.** hug **B.** plain **C.** river **D.** carpet

______ **8.** **A.** delayed **B.** taught **C.** chased **D.** erected

SCORE

Each of your eyes sees things a bit differently. Your brain ___9___ the two pictures so you see only one. Sometimes you can ___10___ a picture in more than one way. Your eyes are tricked into seeing slightly different pictures. When this occurs, your brain gets confused. This is called an optical illusion.

______ **9.** **A.** faces **B.** tastes **C.** dims **D.** blends

______ **10.** **A.** hold **B.** interpret **C.** remove **D.** draw

---

An oasis is an area of lush green ___11___ in a desert. It exists because there is water under the ground. When the water lies close to the surface, an oasis can ___12___.

______ **11.** **A.** air **B.** vegetation **C.** jail **D.** harp

______ **12.** **A.** arise **B.** hurry **C.** fit **D.** drown

---

You know that calculators are well ___13___ because so many people use them. But this was not always the case. Calculators have gone through many ___14___. At first, calculators were large and solved problems slowly. Today they are much smaller and can compute problems quickly.

______ **13.** **A.** launched **B.** poured **C.** accepted **D.** won

______ **14.** **A.** keys **B.** books **C.** parts **D.** stages

---

Agatha Christie wrote about solving strange ___15___. One night she drove off and disappeared. Some people thought Agatha vanished on purpose. Others were puzzled and concerned. Two weeks later the police found Agatha staying at a hotel. She couldn't recall what had happened. She claimed to have lost her ___16___.

______ **15.** **A.** crimes **B.** plants **C.** maps **D.** boxes

______ **16.** **A.** car **B.** memory **C.** glasses **D.** watch

A nebula is a large cloud of dust and gas in space. It is ___1___ within a galaxy. A nebula can be dark, or it can reflect light from stars. These stars can be inside the nebula or in the ___2___ area.

______ **1.** **A.** straight **B.** playful **C.** free **D.** visible

______ **2.** **A.** neighboring **B.** last **C.** ninth **D.** only

---

What animal can eat 50 pounds of food in one sitting? If you said "elephant," you are right, but that little bit isn't dinner. It's more like a ___3___. Can you guess how much food an elephant eats in a day? If you said up to 500 pounds, you have an ___4___ idea of how much it eats.

______ **3.** **A.** drink **B.** friend **C.** snack **D.** foot

______ **4.** **A.** apple **B.** engine **C.** accurate **D.** ill

---

The first human-powered airplane crossed the English Channel in 1979. It looked like a bicycle enclosed in a cabin with long wings. It held just one person. The craft's only power came from the ___5___ of a human. The ___6___ pedaled to turn the propeller that was in the back of the plane.

______ **5.** **A.** muscles **B.** eyes **C.** nerves **D.** thoughts

______ **6.** **A.** engine **B.** pilot **C.** wind **D.** battery

---

Prairie dogs are small, furry animals. They love to play. They live in ___7___ called towns. Prairie dogs build their ___8___ by digging holes and tunnels.

______ **7.** **A.** houses **B.** colonies **C.** toys **D.** plants

______ **8.** **A.** cars **B.** families **C.** hopes **D.** burrows

SCORE

The Everglades extends across the southern tip of Florida. It is a wide-open wetland. It looks like a flooded prairie. But the Everglades consists ___9___ of saw grass. This is not the same as grass on a prairie. The leaves of saw grass have edges that are sharp as a ___10___ blade.

______ **9.** **A.** mainly **B.** quickly **C.** cheaply **D.** flatly

______**10.** **A.** tooth **B.** razor **C.** leather **D.** turnip

---

People once used pools of water as mirrors. Then they saw that ___11___, polished pieces of metal made better mirrors. Later, metallic film was ___12___ to the back of polished plates of glass. This process made the best mirrors.

______**11.** **A.** scratched **B.** smooth **C.** dark **D.** heavy

______**12.** **A.** summoned **B.** led **C.** applied **D.** trotted

---

The hognose snake has a special way to ___13___ itself. It is ___14___ at playing dead. It rolls over on its back. Then it hangs its mouth open. If you turn the snake over on its stomach, it will roll onto its back again.

______**13.** **A.** injure **B.** see **C.** reward **D.** defend

______**14.** **A.** wild **B.** awful **C.** skillful **D.** frisky

---

Marie Curie was a scientist. She wanted to learn more about radioactivity. Marie studied why some things had ___15___ of light that couldn't be seen with the eyes. She tried to help people by using radiation. Marie ___16___ two Nobel Prizes for her work.

______**15.** **A.** beams **B.** maids **C.** years **D.** volumes

______**16.** **A.** sold **B.** ruined **C.** grew **D.** earned

A sea horse is a tiny fish with a long tail. Its head looks like that of a horse. It moves by swimming upright. The sea horse has a single fin on its back that __1__ it through the water. If the sea horse wants to stop, it __2__ its tail around a sea plant.

_____ **1.** **A.** lives **B.** propels **C.** sings **D.** feeds

_____ **2.** **A.** coils **B.** loses **C.** hits **D.** plants

---

Geckos are lizards that are good climbers. There are more than eight hundred varieties of geckos. Many of them make clicking __3__ with their tongues. Others are __4__ and never make any noise.

_____ **3.** **A.** eyes **B.** bites **C.** sounds **D.** leaps

_____ **4.** **A.** tan **B.** tired **C.** nervous **D.** silent

---

There are huge drawings in the desert of Peru. Many are so big that you wouldn't be able to tell what they were if you were standing on the ground. The drawings can be recognized only when __5__ from high above. The Nazca people drew these __6__ many years ago. The reason they were drawn and how they were used are not known.

_____ **5.** **A.** heard **B.** sent **C.** viewed **D.** trapped

_____ **6.** **A.** causes **B.** jobs **C.** designs **D.** reports

---

Wind power is an old __7__ of energy. The windmills used now are much better than they once were. Windmills can supply __8__ power to run lights, toasters, fans, and radios in homes.

_____ **7.** **A.** plan **B.** job **C.** trick **D.** type

_____ **8.** **A.** wave **B.** electrical **C.** solar **D.** no

SCORE

Franklin Chang-Diaz made a big ___9___. He set a goal of flying in space. He trained as a pilot and a scientist. Then Franklin learned how to ___10___ the space shuttle. In 1986 he achieved his goal when he went on a mission in the space shuttle *Columbia*.

______ **9.** **A.** decision **B.** nest **C.** door **D.** hand

______ **10.** **A.** reward **B.** hide **C.** locate **D.** operate

---

Flying squirrels have flaps of skin between their hind and front legs. These flaps can be used like a parachute. The squirrels leap from high branches and ___11___ their flaps of skin. Then they ___12___ through the air to lower branches.

______ **11.** **A.** tear **B.** wrinkle **C.** spread **D.** forget

______ **12.** **A.** trot **B.** soar **C.** freeze **D.** look

---

In 1908 a large crash was heard in a Siberian forest. The cause for this must have been very ___13___. It knocked down trees for miles. The fallen trees all pointed outward in a huge circle. People thought it was a meteor, but there was no ___14___ in the ground.

______ **13.** **A.** weak **B.** powerful **C.** helpful **D.** quiet

______ **14.** **A.** crater **B.** soil **C.** water **D.** tool

---

A hedgehog is an unusual animal. It snorts as it ___15___ for food at night. If it senses danger, the hedgehog will roll into a ball with its spines pointed out. During the day it stays safe in its nest. Sometimes it will ___16___ loudly as it sleeps.

______ **15.** **A.** eats **B.** rummages **C.** melts **D.** dresses

______ **16.** **A.** type **B.** march **C.** snore **D.** eat

The flounder has a body that adapts so it can ___1___ to living on its side. When this type of flatfish is born, it looks like many other fish. Within a short time, the flounder starts to favor one side. One eye will travel slowly ___2___ the head. Then both eyes will be on the same side. Sometimes the mouth will turn upward, too. Finally the flounder will lose all color on its underside.

______ **1.** **A.** dissolve **B.** beg **C.** jerk **D.** convert

______ **2.** **A.** before **B.** from **C.** across **D.** without

---

Daniel Hale Williams was an African American ___3___. He performed a famous heart operation. He ___4___ up a stab wound in a patient's heart and saved the man's life. This had never been done before.

______ **3.** **A.** star **B.** artist **C.** lawyer **D.** surgeon

______ **4.** **A.** worked **B.** ran **C.** stitched **D.** looked

---

The sea otter can use a rock as a tool. First the otter ___5___ in the water on its back. Then it puts a rock on its stomach. Finally the otter takes a clam and ___6___ it against the rock to open it.

______ **5.** **A.** writes **B.** drifts **C.** runs **D.** covers

______ **6.** **A.** eats **B.** rubs **C.** smashes **D.** fishes

---

An alpine glacier is quite a sight. It begins on the side of a mountain. The glacier can be miles long and hundreds of feet ___7___. It looks like a huge river of ___8___ and can fill up an entire valley.

______ **7.** **A.** thick **B.** away **C.** cold **D.** near

______ **8.** **A.** grass **B.** ice **C.** catsup **D.** noise

SCORE

King Tut was a ruler in ancient Egypt. In recent history many people have tried to find the king's burial site. It wasn't until 1922 that his ___9___ was discovered. Inside the sealed entrance were many treasures that had been buried with King Tut. Today these items are on public display at a ___10___ in Cairo, Egypt.

______ **9.** **A.** carnival **B.** tomb **C.** pottery **D.** country

______ **10.** **A.** museum **B.** desert **C.** home **D.** canyon

---

Long ago the people who lived on Easter Island were sculptors. They ___11___ more than 700 huge statues. The statues are 12 feet and 30 feet tall. They ___12___ from 20 to 90 tons. All of the statues have large heads, long ears and arms, but no legs.

______ **11.** **A.** carved **B.** drew **C.** traced **D.** glued

______ **12.** **A.** grow **B.** change **C.** range **D.** lose

---

A total solar eclipse is an amazing ___13___ to witness. It happens when a new moon passes between the sun and Earth. This causes the moon to ___14___ a shadow on Earth. An eclipse like this can be seen from somewhere on Earth at least twice each year.

______ **13.** **A.** match **B.** quiz **C.** occurrence **D.** game

______ **14.** **A.** remove **B.** slip **C.** ask **D.** cast

---

A hologram looks solid like a ___15___ object. But if you try to touch it, you will find that it is not there. The image of the object is ___16___ by a laser beam as a three-dimensional picture.

______ **15.** **A.** fake **B.** broken **C.** liquid **D.** genuine

______ **16.** **A.** eaten **B.** reproduced **C.** burned **D.** melted

The electric eel is a fish. It lives in South American rivers. It has amazing muscles. They make ___1___ of electricity. This fish ___2___ its electricity to defend itself against enemies, catch food, and find its way in the water.

_____ **1.** **A.** chairs **B.** volts **C.** shops **D.** labels

_____ **2.** **A.** fills **B.** ties **C.** discharges **D.** studies

---

Caribou are a type of large deer. The herds migrate long distances. They move across Greenland and the northern ___3___ of North America. They eat many types of plants in open ranges when the weather is warm. At the first ___4___ of winter, they start to move. They go to wooded regions. There they eat small plants. These plants grow on trees and under the snow.

_____ **3.** **A.** echo **B.** package **C.** chain **D.** territory

_____ **4.** **A.** trails **B.** indications **C.** toes **D.** cans

---

The White Horse of Uffington is a carving of a horse. It seems to ___5___ on the British hillside forever. No one has ___6___ to figure out who carved it or why.

_____ **5.** **A.** gallop **B.** iron **C.** bathe **D.** wind

_____ **6.** **A.** crept **B.** said **C.** walked **D.** managed

---

Hulda Crooks had a ___7___ to start climbing mountains at age 66. Then when she was 91 years old, she went to ___8___ Mount Fuji. This is Japan's highest mountain. Hulda climbed slowly to avoid falling. It took her three days to reach the top.

_____ **7.** **A.** legend **B.** price **C.** desire **D.** book

_____ **8.** **A.** drink **B.** belong **C.** scale **D.** lock

SCORE

The first horse lived about 55 million years ago in Europe and North America. It was ten to twenty inches tall. It had a short snout and an arched back. The horse had three toes on its ___9___ feet and four on its front feet. This horse looked very different from today's ___10___ horse.

______ **9.** **A.** hind **B.** gloomy **C.** dirty **D.** fast

______**10.** **A.** ancient **B.** large **C.** dark **D.** open

---

Riding in a hot-air balloon is quiet ___11___ for the noise made by the gas burner. This burner is needed to ___12___ a flame. The flame stretches up into the nylon or polyester bag. This bag is the balloon. The air inside the bag becomes lighter as it is warmed. This causes the balloon to rise. As the air inside the balloon cools, the balloon floats back down to the ground.

______**11.** **A.** above **B.** except **C.** below **D.** in

______**12.** **A.** generate **B.** brush **C.** hug **D.** surprise

---

Sometimes a star will explode. It will become very bright all of a ___13___. Then over a short span of time, it will ___14___ and lose its brightness. This is called a nova.

______**13.** **A.** terrible **B.** certain **C.** sudden **D.** hot

______**14.** **A.** rattle **B.** lighten **C.** improve **D.** dim

---

New Zealand is a country consisting of two ___15___ islands. It is known for the ___16___ of its waterfalls, lakes, beaches, green lowlands, and snow-capped mountains.

______**15.** **A.** naughty **B.** rubber **C.** weak **D.** principal

______**16.** **A.** year **B.** hollow **C.** beauty **D.** dawn

Some people say that they have seen a strange beast in the Pacific Northwest. They ___1___ it as looking like a huge ape. These people say that it walks on two legs, like a human. Some people ___2___ that this creature is Bigfoot. But most scientists are not sure if Bigfoot really exists.

_____ **1.** **A.** argue **B.** type **C.** describe **D.** join

_____ **2.** **A.** storm **B.** row **C.** melt **D.** claim

---

Crystals grow in a ___3___ pattern. They have smooth, flat surfaces that join to make sharp edges. Snowflakes, sugar, salt, rocks, and metals are things that are ___4___ of crystals.

_____ **3.** **A.** quiet **B.** regular **C.** loud **D.** tan

_____ **4.** **A.** composed **B.** talk **C.** shower **D.** asleep

---

After hatching, a bird becomes strongly attached to the thing that is closest to it. This is called imprinting. It ___5___ that a baby bird will follow its mother. But a little bird imprints on other things if its mother isn't in the ___6___ when it hatches. A baby bird can imprint on a balloon, a box, or a person.

_____ **5.** **A.** ties **B.** asks **C.** ensures **D.** fills

_____ **6.** **A.** pond **B.** mall **C.** vicinity **D.** television

---

Carlsbad Caverns are famous caves. They are located in southeastern New Mexico. In warm ___7___ millions of bats fly out of the caves at dusk. They go out ___8___ insects to eat.

_____ **7.** **A.** boards **B.** weather **C.** faucets **D.** maps

_____ **8.** **A.** hunting **B.** flying **C.** trusting **D.** placing

SCORE

In the North American Great Plains, there are stones that form the shape of wheels with spokes. They are called medicine wheels. The stones point to the sun and ___9___ stars. It is thought that Native Americans once used the wheels as calendars. Special ___10___ were marked on these calendars.

______ **9.** **A.** playful **B.** wise **C.** blind **D.** specific

______ **10.** **A.** fires **B.** fish **C.** barrels **D.** celebrations

---

Thomas Greene Bethune, a blind African American slave, played the piano. Although blind, he had an ___11___ talent. He started writing music at the age of five. Thomas is ___12___ as a great musician. Yet the money he earned went to his owner.

______ **11.** **A.** asking **B.** amazing **C.** icy **D.** eating

______ **12.** **A.** ranked **B.** lost **C.** bent **D.** forced

---

A platypus is an odd animal. It is ___13___ at ease on land or in the streams and lakes of Australia. The platypus swims to catch its food. The platypus uses its duck-like, ___14___ front feet and its long, flat tail to swim. It sleeps in a burrow on shore.

______ **13.** **A.** tall **B.** giant **C.** equally **D.** heavy

______ **14.** **A.** hot **B.** webbed **C.** tied **D.** icy

---

The tuatara looks like a lizard. It ___15___ to a group of reptiles that lived millions of years ago. The others of its kind are dead. But the tuatara continues to ___16___ on some of the smaller islands of New Zealand.

______ **15.** **A.** pretends **B.** sits **C.** belongs **D.** gets

______ **16.** **A.** thrive **B.** buy **C.** forget **D.** discover

The sloth lives in the Central and South American forests. Its shaggy, grayish-green hair helps it hide in the trees. The sloth has curved claws. It can hang upside down on a branch. It __1__ on fruit, leaves, and twigs. The sloth moves at a very slow pace. It drinks dew or raindrops when it is __2__.

______ **1.** **A.** nibbles **B.** dances **C.** winks **D.** fixes

______ **2.** **A.** asleep **B.** tired **C.** brave **D.** thirsty

---

King Cheops of ancient Egypt had the Great Pyramid built. He wanted it to be his tomb. It took about twenty years to __3__. In that time many thousands of people worked on it in the desert heat. They had to cut and transport the huge stone blocks for the pyramid. The workers lifted these __4__ blocks without the help of modern machines.

______ **3.** **A.** support **B.** construct **C.** lose **D.** soak

______ **4.** **A.** tiny **B.** small **C.** gray **D.** enormous

---

A big star can __5__, leaving tiny bits behind. At times the bits come together and spin __6__. The bits make up a star. This star is called a pulsar. It sends out flashes of light as it spins.

______ **5.** **A.** grab **B.** freeze **C.** explode **D.** decide

______ **6.** **A.** swiftly **B.** early **C.** soon **D.** usually

---

Angel Falls is in Venezuela. It's the highest waterfall in the world. It is in an area of __7__ cliffs. The falls __8__ from a cliff surrounded by the beauty of the rain forest.

______ **7.** **A.** glass **B.** steep **C.** electric **D.** oak

______ **8.** **A.** stamp **B.** know **C.** drop **D.** invite

SCORE

Texans fought a war to become free. A Hispanic woman, Andrea Castañon Ramirez Candaläria, was a nurse. She worked at a Texas mission ___9___ the Alamo. She ___10___ for the injured men. Andrea was wounded in the war, but she survived. She lived to be 113 years old.

______ **9.** **A.** called **B.** carved **C.** stored **D.** won

______ **10.** **A.** held **B.** cared **C.** asked **D.** touched

---

A sponge lives at the bottom of the sea. A sponge will not die if it is cut into ___11___. Each section will grow new body parts. A sponge's body ___12___ many holes. Water takes air and food through these holes.

______ **11.** **A.** animals **B.** bins **C.** pieces **D.** stories

______ **12.** **A.** rewards **B.** contains **C.** eats **D.** whispers

---

The international date line helps us keep up with dates around the world. This is ___13___ because Earth's spin makes midnight, the start of a new day, occur at different times in different places. You can take a ___14___ around the world. You lose a day going west and gain a day going east.

______ **13.** **A.** careless **B.** told **C.** calm **D.** essential

______ **14.** **A.** stone **B.** trip **C.** glove **D.** clap

---

Falling objects are pulled down by gravity. A parachute slows down this fall. In an ___15___ a person safely jumps from a plane using a parachute. ___16___ such as food can also be easily dropped.

______ **15.** **A.** acre **B.** issue **C.** emergency **D.** empty

______ **16.** **A.** Goods **B.** News **C.** Water **D.** Facts

A rainbow is seen when the sun's rays shine on drops of rain or mist. It appears in the sky __1__ the sun. It has seven colors. The amount of space used by each color __2__ on the size of the waterdrops in the rainbow.

_____ **1.** **A.** gold **B.** opposite **C.** water **D.** upset

_____ **2.** **A.** quits **B.** blends **C.** sits **D.** depends

---

The giant sequoia is a tree. It once grew all over the northern half of the world. Now it grows just on the western __3__ of California's mountains. This very old evergreen has a wide base. It is also very tall. In many __4__ lightning has destroyed the top of the tree because of its height.

_____ **3.** **A.** joys **B.** plains **C.** slopes **D.** coasts

_____ **4.** **A.** cases **B.** axes **C.** repairs **D.** facts

---

A hovercraft is a vehicle that __5__ on a layer of air above land or water. The air __6__ is made using fans. There is a rubber skirt on the craft's lower edge. It fills with air from the fans. This helps the craft cross rough ground or waves.

_____ **5.** **A.** moves **B.** sews **C.** feeds **D.** crashes

_____ **6.** **A.** show **B.** pill **C.** cushion **D.** stem

---

Banff is Canada's oldest national park. It is visited by many __7__. They come to see how glaciers have shaped the park's deep valleys and lakes over the last million years. Glaciers that are still __8__ in the snow-capped mountains can also be viewed.

_____ **7.** **A.** stones **B.** tourists **C.** soldiers **D.** areas

_____ **8.** **A.** heard **B.** repeated **C.** believed **D.** present

SCORE

Satellites have been sent into space to ___9___ Earth. They have been made for different ___10___. Some satellites help us communicate with other people in the world. Others help us study the weather or changes on Earth's surface.

______ **9.** **A.** fix **B.** turn **C.** enter **D.** orbit

______ **10.** **A.** models **B.** reasons **C.** acts **D.** traps

---

In 1910 Madame C. J. Walker ___11___ a line of cosmetic products. As her ___12___ grew, she started many beauty schools. She was the first African American woman to become a millionaire.

______ **11.** **A.** helped **B.** baked **C.** manufactured **D.** piled

______ **12.** **A.** business **B.** appetite **C.** show **D.** comfort

---

In 1520 Ferdinand Magellan set a ___13___ to find the Pacific. As he searched, he sailed to the southern end of South America. There Magellan saw a group of islands. Large fires burned on the shores. He named the ___14___ Tierra del Fuego, or Land of Fire.

______ **13.** **A.** course **B.** fort **C.** bird **D.** child

______ **14.** **A.** face **B.** region **C.** task **D.** minute

---

There's an old tale about a large island. It is said to have been located in the Atlantic Ocean. This island was called Atlantis. A strong ___15___ ruled the island. Its armies tried to conquer both Greece and Egypt, but they lost. Later this island sank due to volcanic eruptions, earthquakes, and ___16___ from a tidal wave.

______ **15.** **A.** statue **B.** building **C.** chat **D.** empire

______ **16.** **A.** news **B.** tracks **C.** floods **D.** avenues

There is just one diamond mine in the United States. This natural ___1___ is located in Arkansas. Thousands of diamonds have been found there. These gems are small but ___2___.

______ **1.** **A.** enemy **B.** scale **C.** wonder **D.** stripe

______ **2.** **A.** cozy **B.** foggy **C.** bold **D.** perfect

---

Many cave paintings have been ___3___. They give us clues to the past. They date back to prehistoric times. Some have been well preserved because the ___4___ to the caves were sealed.

______ **3.** **A.** attacked **B.** lit **C.** sold **D.** found

______ **4.** **A.** keys **B.** entrances **C.** messages **D.** paints

---

A crowd of ___5___ cheered as Rick Hanson returned from his trip around the world. He had spent the last two years pushing himself in his wheelchair to make this journey. Rick had faced many hardships, but he never quit. He wanted to prove that a person with a disability can ___6___ a difficult goal.

______ **5.** **A.** stamps **B.** dens **C.** lists **D.** fans

______ **6.** **A.** achieve **B.** smother **C.** view **D.** spend

---

A sand dollar is an animal that lives in shallow waters off the coast. It stays partly ___7___ in the sand. It crawls and digs using the little spines on its body. The sand dollar finds bits of food to eat while it digs in the ___8___ of sand.

______ **7.** **A.** buried **B.** cut **C.** neat **D.** sewn

______ **8.** **A.** hearts **B.** tins **C.** grains **D.** castles

SCORE

The Yukon is a mountainous region. It's found in Canada. Many people once came to this area in ___9___ of gold. Now only ___10___ of this wild gold rush are left.

______ 9. A. canoe B. pursuit C. art D. tag

______10. A. traces B. islands C. days D. files

The first American woman to travel in space was Sally Ride. She went in the space shuttle for a six-day ___11___. Sally helped launch satellites, and she ___12___ experiments.

______11. A. mission B. sleep C. leap D. walk

______12. A. obeyed B. dyed C. conducted D. sealed

Long ago the giant panda was a common sight. It lived in many parts of China. Then people began cutting down ___13___ areas of bamboo. The giant panda had a hard time finding bamboo to eat. Now the giant panda lives only high in the mountains of southeastern China. People are working to protect the giant panda. But today seeing a giant panda is very ___14___.

______13. A. easy B. slight C. dangerous D. immense

______14. A. purple B. dry C. uncommon D. large

A robot is a machine. It is built to do certain ___15___. A computer inside the robot gives it directions about how to complete special jobs. A robot is faster and makes fewer ___16___ than most people.

______15. A. flips B. tasks C. flowers D. calls

______16. A. laws B. sleeves C. shouts D. mistakes

The sea is salty. Many types of salts are ___1___ in the water and make it this way. The most common type of salt in the sea is table salt. Underwater volcanoes are the ___2___ of some salts in the sea. Other salts are carried from rocks to the sea by rivers.

______ **1.** **A.** dissolved **B.** exported **C.** worn **D.** rescued

______ **2.** **A.** well **B.** question **C.** origin **D.** envelope

---

The Arctic Circle is close to the North Pole. It doesn't have a day and night ___3___ like most places do. This is because it is so far north. For six months the sun never sets below the ___4___. For the following six months of the year, the sky remains dark except for light from the moon and the stars.

______ **3.** **A.** vacation **B.** tub **C.** song **D.** cycle

______ **4.** **A.** wall **B.** skyline **C.** end **D.** general

---

The manatee lives in freshwater canals. It's a mammal, but it spends its entire life in the water. The manatee helps keep the canals ___5___. It eats large amounts of plants that cause ___6___ in the canal.

______ **5.** **A.** happy **B.** kind **C.** clear **D.** loud

______ **6.** **A.** blocks **B.** signs **C.** wagons **D.** tables

---

A frilled lizard looks odd. It has a piece of skin around its neck. This is called a frill. When this lizard becomes ___7___, it will try to run. If it can't run, the lizard will ___8___ its frill, hiss, and scare its enemy.

______ **7.** **A.** sleepy **B.** jolly **C.** perfect **D.** frightened

______ **8.** **A.** cut **B.** lift **C.** answer **D.** plow

SCORE

Years ago some people ____9____ the 24 time zones around the world. The prime meridian, a line of longitude, was ____10____ as the starting point. A one-hour difference was set between zones. But every place in a zone had the same time.

______ **9.** **A.** devised **B.** bent **C.** saluted **D.** felt

______**10.** **A.** broken **B.** chosen **C.** lost **D.** hidden

---

Corals live in the ocean. They like waters that are warm, clear, and shallow. Corals ____11____ their hard coverings together. They form structures called reefs. These coverings stay together even after the animals die. Coral reefs can be found near the shores of tropical ____12____.

______**11.** **A.** stop **B.** pit **C.** guard **D.** link

______**12.** **A.** islands **B.** fences **C.** fish **D.** days

---

A glider is a type of aircraft. It looks like a plane, but it doesn't have a motor. Usually a plane is used to tow the glider into the sky. The glider is ____13____ when the plane lets go. Then the glider flies in flows of air called air ____14____.

______**13.** **A.** chased **B.** eyed **C.** launched **D.** nailed

______**14.** **A.** nations **B.** currents **C.** pears **D.** orders

---

The Great Enclosure was a huge group of buildings, corridors, and courtyards. It stood in the African desert during ancient times. Today scholars study the ____15____ that remain. But the reason the complex was built is still a ____16____.

______**15.** **A.** tapes **B.** cubs **C.** deserts **D.** ruins

______**16.** **A.** hunt **B.** wish **C.** puzzle **D.** mud

Read each paragraph. Write a word that makes sense on each line.

Aisha was starting to walk home from school when it began to rain. "Oh, no," she thought. "I forgot to bring my **(1)** ________________. Now my **(2)** ________________ will get soaked!"

Cody had always wanted to be in the band. He dreamed of playing a big **(3)** ________________. He was sure that no one would be able to **(4)** ________________ better than he could.

Last spring I tried to build a birdhouse. I used a hammer and some **(5)** ________________. When I finished, that birdhouse looked **(6)** ________________.

To check your answers, turn to page 60.

Read each paragraph. Write a sentence that makes sense on each line.

Mrs. Singh was planting flowers when her spade struck something hard. She wondered what she should do next. **(1)** ______________________________.
She gasped in surprise when she saw what the object was. **(2)** ______________________________.
Mrs. Singh knew just what she would do with it.
(3) ______________________________.

Carmen needed to earn some money. She really loved animals. What could she do? **(4)** ______________
______________________________.
Then her next-door neighbor, Ms. Fielder, rang the doorbell. **(5)** ______________________________.
Now Carmen has a job, even though it has nothing to do with animals. **(6)** ______________
______________________________.

To check your answers, turn to page 60.

Most people like football because it is full of action. But the ball is in motion only twenty percent of the game. The rest of the time is **expended** in things such as huddles and time-outs.

______ **1.** In this paragraph, the word **expended** means

A. kicked
B. spent
C. wished
D. saved

Many towns have **quaint** names. Some odd ones are Darling, Lemon, and Soso in Mississippi. The town of Licking is in Ohio. And you'll find Snowflake in Arizona.

______ **2.** In this paragraph, the word **quaint** means

A. unusual
B. long
C. southern
D. regular

The squid is a sea animal with ten **tentacles**. It uses eight of them to catch its food. The other two are longer. The squid uses them to bring the food to its mouth.

______ **3.** In this paragraph, the word **tentacles** means

A. eyes
B. arms
C. nets
D. heads

The deepest lake in the world is found in Russia. It is more than five thousand feet deep. Its great depth **surpasses** the height of some mountains.

______ **4.** In this paragraph, the word **surpasses** means

A. shines above
B. loses
C. appears
D. goes beyond

SCORE

You can measure yourself. On bare feet, stand with your back to a wall. Put a thin piece of cardboard across the top of your head and mark where it hits the wall. Run a tape measure from the mark to the floor. Now you know **precisely** how tall you are.

______ **5.** In this paragraph, the word **precisely** means

A. partly **C.** exactly
B. slightly **D.** fairly

The rose has long been a sign of **secrecy**. Hundreds of years ago, people wore roses behind their ears. It meant that the people wearing the roses had heard something, but would not tell what they had heard.

______ **6.** In this paragraph, the word **secrecy** means

A. riddles **C.** talking
B. silence **D.** sharing

Paul Cézanne was a famous French painter. It is said that he worked very slowly. Since one of his favorite subjects was fruit, it often **perished** before he finished. So Cézanne began painting fruit made of wax instead.

______ **7.** In this paragraph, the word **perished** means

A. spoiled **C.** fell
B. was eaten **D.** grew

How can anybody remain underwater for ten minutes? **Ponder** that question no more. Just fill a glass with water. Then hold it over your head for ten minutes!

______ **8.** In this paragraph, the word **ponder** means

A. swim after **C.** forget about
B. think about **D.** know of

How do pilots avoid **collisions** with other planes in the air? The sky is mapped into highways just like the land is. Signals are sent up from control towers to mark these "skyways." It's a pilot's job to listen to the signals.

_____ **1.** In this paragraph, the word **collisions** means

A. birds **C.** insects
B. crashes **D.** tires

A **cavern** is a hole in the surface of Earth made by the forces of nature. People like to explore and hide things in these dark rooms and tunnels under the ground.

_____ **2.** In this paragraph, the word **cavern** means

A. pool **C.** cave
B. house **D.** bump

Sand that sits on top of clay in streams is called quicksand. The quicksand is **saturated** with water because the water cannot drain through the clay.

_____ **3.** In this paragraph, the word **saturated** means

A. tired **C.** dried
B. reached **D.** soaked

The Venus's-flytrap is a plant that **consumes** bugs. When there are no bugs, this plant will gladly accept bits of cheese!

_____ **4.** In this paragraph, the word **consumes** means

A. eats **C.** hates
B. releases **D.** grows

SCORE

The trunk of a tree is made up of **annual** rings. Each year a new layer of wood grows to form a new ring. You can tell the age of a tree by counting its rings.

______ **5.** In this paragraph, the word **annual** means

A. yearly **C.** hard
B. large **D.** weekly

Food on the frontier was simple. People ate many things made from flour. Flour was **nourishing** and did not spoil. Foods made from flour gave people energy to work hard.

______ **6.** In this paragraph, the word **nourishing** means

A. cheerful **C.** difficult
B. healthful **D.** expensive

We all have muscles **attached** to our outer ears. Some people work hard at moving these muscles. These are the people who can wiggle their ears! Can you do it?

______ **7.** In this paragraph, the word **attached** means

A. developed **C.** adjusted
B. connected **D.** chosen

Faith Ringgold writes children's books and draws **illustrations** for them. Her special art form is story quilts. She sews together patches of cloth that have words and drawings. Put together, they tell a story.

______ **8.** In this paragraph, the word **illustrations** means

A. pictures **C.** blankets
B. artists **D.** pencils

Gertrude Ederle was the first woman to swim the English Channel. On August 6, 1926, she jumped into the icy water. As she swam, it began to storm. She could have **discontinued** her swim. But Gertrude would not give up. She finished in 14 hours and 31 minutes.

_____ **1.** In this paragraph, the word **discontinued** means

A. sped up
B. changed
C. stopped
D. timed

The sound of a person's voice is **related** to the length of his or her vocal cords. Most men have deeper voices than women. That's because men's vocal cords are longer. A tall person often has a deeper voice than a short person.

_____ **2.** In this paragraph, the word **related** means

A. dependent on
B. hidden from
C. said
D. compared to

When a whip is snapped, it makes a loud cracking sound. Whips can **accelerate** to a speed of more than seven hundred miles per hour. At that speed a whip can break the sound barrier.

_____ **3.** In this paragraph, the word **accelerate** means

A. maintain
B. speed up
C. go slower
D. remain the same

Surgeons wore white uniforms until 1914. A doctor thought that the white uniform showed too much blood from **operations**. He wore green instead. Red did not show as much on the green.

_____ **4.** In this paragraph, the word **operations** means

A. surgeries
B. janitors
C. oxygen
D. straps

SCORE

There is only one flock of whooping cranes in the world. These **endangered** birds live in Canada. They migrate to Texas for the winter. If all the birds in this flock die, the whooping crane will become extinct.

______ **5.** In this paragraph, the word **endangered** means

A. large | **C.** threatened
B. white | **D.** Canadian

Isamu Noguchi studied to be a doctor. What he really enjoyed was art. The sculptures he made are famous. Noguchi's love of art **endured** through his whole life.

______ **6.** In this paragraph, the word **endured** means

A. started | **C.** ended
B. painted | **D.** lasted

In Rome long ago, only the emperor and his family could wear purple. Others were **forbidden** to wear that color!

______ **7.** In this paragraph, the word **forbidden** means

A. chosen | **C.** encouraged
B. spoken | **D.** not allowed

On the tip of each finger is a pattern of ridges. This pattern is called a fingerprint. Each finger has a **distinct** fingerprint. No two people in the world have the same fingerprints. A person's fingerprints always remain the same—they never change.

______ **8.** In this paragraph, the word **distinct** means

A. particular | **C.** smooth
B. silver | **D.** funny

The tortoise is the animal that lives the longest. The Mauritius tortoise had a life **span** of 152 years. Some scientists think it lived for 200 years! The Carolina tortoise is found in the United States. Some of these creatures have lived for 123 years.

_____ **1.** In this paragraph, the word **span** means

- **A.** height
- **B.** weight
- **C.** length
- **D.** thirst

A snake has no legs, but it can crawl. There are broad scales on the underside of a snake. It can move each scale independently. When each scale pushes against a spot in the ground, the snake moves **forward**.

_____ **2.** In this paragraph, the word **forward** means

- **A.** tomorrow
- **B.** second
- **C.** inside
- **D.** ahead

Nancy Lopez started playing golf when she was eight. Her dad, Domingo Lopez, taught her. She practiced hard and **dedicated** much of her time to her sport. Nancy Lopez became one of the greatest women golfers. She has been named to golf's Hall of Fame.

_____ **3.** In this paragraph, the word **dedicated** means

- **A.** gave
- **B.** dreamed
- **C.** rested
- **D.** spoke

In 1900 Johann Huslinger traveled from Vienna to Paris. That is a distance of 871 miles. Johann **hiked** for 55 days. He went the whole way on his hands!

_____ **4.** In this paragraph, the word **hiked** means

- **A.** laughed
- **B.** lifted
- **C.** walked
- **D.** raced

SCORE

What makes popcorn pop? Popcorn kernels are small and hard. There is water within the kernel. When the moisture heats up, it turns to **steam**. The steam causes the kernel to explode.

______ **5.** In this paragraph, the word **steam** means

A. dry corn
B. water vapor
C. melted butter
D. sea salt

Many people believe that red makes a bull angry and causes him to attack. That is why a bullfighter waves a red cape. But a bull is colorblind. It is the **motion** of the cape that excites the bull. A bullfighter could wave a white or green cape, and the bull would charge.

______ **6.** In this paragraph, the word **motion** means

A. color
B. red
C. stopping
D. shaking

Only one bird can fly **backward**. It is the tiny hummingbird. The bird flies in front of a flower. It sucks the nectar out of the flower. When it is finished, it simply backs up.

______ **7.** In this paragraph, the word **backward** means

A. in reverse
B. fast
C. up and down
D. like a helicopter

In shot-putting, the shot used by men weighs 16 pounds. The one used by women weighs 9 pounds. Each **competitor** throws the shot from a circle to a special landing area. The winner is the one who throws the shot the farthest.

______ **8.** In this paragraph, the word **competitor** means

A. player
B. winner
C. audience
D. special equipment

Some people think the boa constrictor is the longest snake. But they are wrong. This snake **approaches** 16 feet. But the regal python can grow to a length of 35 feet. It is the longest snake known. But it is not the heaviest snake. The anaconda weighs 100 pounds more than the python. It can weigh 360 pounds.

_____ **1.** In this paragraph, the word **approaches** means

A. is exactly
B. is far from
C. comes close to
D. is greater than

Giuseppe Verdi was a famous **composer**. When he was young, he could not go to the music school in Milan, Italy. The teachers said he lacked talent. After he became famous, the school changed its name. It became the Verdi Conservatory of Music.

_____ **2.** In this paragraph, the word **composer** means

A. cook
B. music writer
C. listener
D. pupil

How can you tell a vegetable from a fruit? In 1893 the Supreme Court passed **judgment** on the subject. If it is consumed with the main course of a meal, it's a vegetable. If it is served as a dessert or snack, it's a fruit.

_____ **3.** In this paragraph, the word **judgment** means

A. properties
B. award
C. decision
D. umpire

During the 1800s miners took canaries into the mines. If the canaries stopped singing, the miners knew the supply of air was almost **exhausted**. The canaries warned the miners.

_____ **4.** In this paragraph, the word **exhausted** means

A. used up
B. designed
C. invented
D. explored

SCORE

Dragonflies are usually seen flying through the air. But this is during the last stage of a dragonfly's life. It can only fly for a few weeks. It spends most of its life underwater. Before becoming an **adult**, it lives underwater as a nymph. A nymph looks like a mature dragonfly. But it does not have wings.

______ **5.** In this paragraph, the word **adult** means

A. baby
B. tame
C. young
D. full-grown

When you yawn, your mouth opens. You take in a large **quantity** of air. A yawn is refreshing. It may stop you from dropping off to sleep.

______ **6.** In this paragraph, the word **quantity** means

A. present
B. voice
C. amount
D. song

Blue whales are the largest animals that have ever lived. Newborn blue whales are **gigantic**. A baby blue whale is 25 feet long at birth. That's the size of a house!

______ **7.** In this paragraph, the word **gigantic** means

A. small
B. very large
C. a kind of fish
D. able to swim

Ice cream was first made in China. The explorer Marco Polo described eating dishes of ice **flavored** with fruit. Italians liked it so much they changed the name to Italian ices. The French added cream and renamed it ice cream.

______ **8.** In this paragraph, the word **flavored** means

A. given warmth
B. given taste
C. given cream
D. given dishes

Lorraine Hansberry wrote the play *A Raisin in the Sun*. It is about an African American family that wants to **relocate** to a white neighborhood. The move brings out the love and strength in the family. *A Raisin in the Sun* was the first play on Broadway written by an African American woman.

______ **1.** In this paragraph, the word **relocate** means

- **A.** visit
- **B.** write a play
- **C.** move to a new place
- **D.** stay away from

Colorado got its name from a Spanish word. The Spanish word *colorado* means "red." Spanish explorers found a river with reddish-colored water. They **declared** it the Colorado River. The state got its name from the river.

______ **2.** In this paragraph, the word **declared** means

- **A.** swam in
- **B.** colored
- **C.** discovered
- **D.** made it known as

Albert Von Tilzer must have been very **creative**. He wrote the song "Take Me Out to the Ball Game." But Albert had never been to a baseball game. He did not even like the sport! He wrote the song by thinking about how much fun a game might be.

______ **3.** In this paragraph, the word **creative** means

- **A.** dull
- **B.** athletic
- **C.** a baseball fan
- **D.** able to imagine

Mistletoe has thick green leaves and white berries. It is never found growing on the ground. This plant does not grow in soil. It grows on the **limbs** of trees.

______ **4.** In this paragraph, the word **limbs** means

- **A.** clouds
- **B.** branches
- **C.** roots
- **D.** flowers

SCORE

Ping-Pong is another name for table tennis. Ping-Pong and tennis are very much **alike**. In both games a ball is hit over a net. The name Ping-Pong came from the noise made when the ball was hit by a paddle.

______ **5.** In this paragraph, the word **alike** means

A. different

B. sounds like

C. hard

D. the same

Pulse is measured by feeling for the **throb** in a person's wrist. The number of throbs is counted for one minute. A pulse is waves of blood. Each wave is moving from the heart through the wrist.

______ **6.** In this paragraph, the word **throb** means

A. loud noise

B. beat

C. wrinkle

D. measure of time

The Grand Canyon is the longest gorge in the world. It is more than 200 miles long. In some places this **scenic** canyon is one mile deep. It is as much as 18 miles wide. It was formed by the Colorado River cutting deep into the land.

______ **7.** In this paragraph, the word **scenic** means

A. beautiful

B. boring

C. ordinary

D. frightening

The giraffe is the tallest animal in the world. It can grow to a height of twenty feet. Giraffes **tower** over people and cars.

______ **8.** In this paragraph, the word **tower** means

A. run from

B. stand tall

C. knock down

D. work hard

Lewis and Clark explored the American West. Sacagawea was their guide. She was **capable** of speaking to many Native American tribes. She got the supplies the explorers needed for their trip.

______ **1.** In this paragraph, the word **capable** means

A. sharp **C.** able
B. tired **D.** afraid

The Blue Grotto has many **visitors**. This popular cave was carved by ocean waves. It's on the island of Capri. The sun reflects off the water outside the cave. This makes a blue glow in the cave.

______ **2.** In this paragraph, the word **visitors** means

A. guests **C.** bears
B. records **D.** insects

Dingoes are wild dogs in Australia. No one knows how they got there. The people who moved to the area long ago might have had dogs. Dingoes may be **descendants** of these dogs.

______ **3.** In this paragraph, the word **descendants** means

A. details **C.** parents
B. offspring **D.** worlds

A horned toad is a lizard. Sharp spines cover its body for protection. But if a foe does **pounce** on the horned toad, the toad can squirt blood from its eyes. Then the attacker runs away.

______ **4.** In this paragraph, the word **pounce** means

A. behave **C.** march
B. trust **D.** jump

SCORE

The praying mantis is a fierce insect. It **ceases** to move so that it looks like part of a plant. The mantis uses its front legs to trap its prey. It usually catches insects, small frogs, and lizards.

______ **5.** In this paragraph, the word **ceases** means

A. quits **C.** feeds
B. inspects **D.** whistles

In ancient times the Egyptians built a huge lighthouse. The base was a fortress where the soldiers lived. At the top of the tower, a **bonfire** burned brightly all night. The flames could be seen from far away. Sailors found their way home safely.

______ **6.** In this paragraph, the word **bonfire** means

A. small flare **C.** huge light bulb
B. match **D.** large fire

Mary Fields escaped from slavery. She went to Montana. Mary became an **accomplished** stage driver and delivered the mail. She drove her mail route even in the worst weather.

______ **7.** In this paragraph, the word **accomplished** means

A. wild **C.** expert
B. hopeful **D.** pretend

Saint Elmo's Fire is sometimes seen around ships during storms. It is a round **burst** of light that looks like fire. But it is caused by electricity from storms.

______ **8.** In this paragraph, the word **burst** means

A. cone **C.** stream
B. explosion **D.** disaster

The Great Sphinx was made for a king of ancient Egypt. Its head was carved to look like that of the king. However, it has a lion's body. This **symbolized** the king's strength.

______ **1.** In this paragraph, the word **symbolized** means

A. held up **C.** ran from
B. took over **D.** stood for

The cone snail has a beautiful marbled shell. Many people like to collect the shell. But they must be careful of a living cone snail because it has poisoned **barbs**. The snail's stab is fatal.

______ **2.** In this paragraph, the word **barbs** means

A. rounded tips **C.** sharp points
B. golden crowns **D.** dull edges

Libby Riddles wanted to win a famous sled-dog race in Alaska. She knew conditions would be **brutal**, but the blizzards and freezing weather did not stop her. She became the first woman to win the race.

______ **3.** In this paragraph, the word **brutal** means

A. simple **C.** ordinary
B. easy **D.** cruel

Some museums exhibit animal bones. Museum workers must clean the bones **prior** to putting them on display. The workers use dermestid beetles. The beetles can clean the bones without hurting them.

______ **4.** In this paragraph, the word **prior** means

A. now **C.** later
B. before **D.** during

SCORE

Laura Bridgman had a **grave** illness when she was a child. It caused her to lose her sight and hearing. She went to a school for the blind in Boston. There she learned many things.

______ **5.** In this paragraph, the word **grave** means

A. serious
B. excellent
C. mild
D. simple

The porcupine fish can make itself look very odd. If it senses danger, it takes a breath of air and puffs out its body. Then it looks like a spine-covered ball. When the danger passes, the fish **deflates** itself.

______ **6.** In this paragraph, the word **deflates** means

A. swims away from
B. releases air from
C. moves close to
D. pushes spines through

Electric cars are an old idea. But they may be a part of our **future**. They run well and do not pollute the air. They have been improved since they were first invented. They run faster and don't need to be recharged as often.

______ **7.** In this paragraph, the word **future** means

A. time past
B. now
C. present
D. time ahead

The Dead Sea is **positioned** between Israel and Jordan. The sea got its name because birds do not fly over it. They cannot find any food there. Fish cannot live in the water. It is too salty.

______ **8.** In this paragraph, the word **positioned** means

A. for now
B. without doubt
C. in place
D. at work

Ayers Rock is in Australia. Many tourists come to see and climb this huge rock formation. It stands in sharp **contrast** to the flat desert country around it.

_____ **1.** In this paragraph, the word **contrast** means

A. difference
B. balance
C. similarity
D. introduction

Tundra is found in the far north or on high mountaintops. The **soil** is almost always frozen. Trees cannot grow in those cold, dry regions. But mosses, lichens, and grasses can grow there.

_____ **2.** In this paragraph, the word **soil** means

A. mill
B. planet
C. water
D. earth

The pygmy marmoset lives in Brazil's forests. It is the smallest monkey. Its head and body are about six inches long. You can **barely** feel its fur because its coat is so fine.

_____ **3.** In this paragraph, the word **barely** means

A. coldly
B. hardly
C. lively
D. sweetly

Pocahontas was just a young girl. But she **pleaded** with her father to save a man's life. Her father, the chief, did not kill him. The man she saved was Captain John Smith. He was leader of the Jamestown colony.

_____ **4.** In this paragraph, the word **pleaded** means

A. begged
B. loved
C. searched
D. hid

SCORE

The Leaning Tower of Pisa is in Italy. The ground on one side of the tower is so soft that the side is **sinking**. This makes the tower lean a tiny bit more each year. People are trying to save it from falling.

______ **5.** In this paragraph, the word **sinking** means

A. rising higher **C.** dropping lower
B. walking with **D.** touching against

A group of Native Americans once built their homes in Colorado's canyon walls. But the cliff dwellers left their homes because of a **prolonged** drought. They had to find a place with more water.

______ **6.** In this paragraph, the word **prolonged** means

A. long **C.** short
B. unimportant **D.** loud

A comet is made of frozen gases, ice, and dust. It **revolves** around the sun. As it comes closer to the sun, some of it melts. This melted part becomes the tail of the comet.

______ **7.** In this paragraph, the word **revolves** means

A. grabs **C.** listens
B. climbs **D.** circles

The Red Sea is a **descriptive** name for the body of water between Africa and Asia. The hills near it are reddish. The coral reefs, seaweed, and tiny sea animals are red, too.

______ **8.** In this paragraph, the word **descriptive** means

A. imaginary **C.** unlikely
B. ridiculous **D.** picturing in words

Mercury is a metal that stays liquid whether it is hot or cold. Mercury is used inside a **thermometer**. It can show if you are running a fever.

_____ **1.** In this paragraph, the word **thermometer** means

A. tool that cleans teeth
B. tool that weeds gardens
C. tool that measures hot and cold
D. tool that shows speeds

Sometimes it looks as if there is a ring of light shining around the moon. This is **actually** from clouds high in Earth's atmosphere. The clouds have bits of ice that bend and scatter the moonlight. This is usually a sign that a storm is coming.

_____ **2.** In this paragraph, the word **actually** means

A. suddenly
B. really
C. exactly
D. quickly

The black mamba is a snake. It lives in Africa. The mamba has a bad temper and will attack if it is disturbed. A very small amount of its venom can be **fatal** to a person.

_____ **3.** In this paragraph, the word **fatal** means

A. causing death
B. making wrong
C. getting well
D. seeming happy

Koko, a gorilla, was taught how to communicate using sign language. She asked for a kitten for her birthday. Koko carefully **attended** to her kitten. She talked to it using the signs.

_____ **4.** In this paragraph, the word **attended** means

A. worked together
B. took care of
C. kept apart from
D. provided money for

SCORE

Mount Mazama is a volcano in Oregon. It has been **inactive** for years. The edges of the crater have fallen in. The crater has filled up with water. It is now known as Crater Lake.

______ **5.** In this paragraph, the word **inactive** means

A. upset **C.** alive
B. quiet **D.** stubborn

Dorothea Dix worked hard. She improved life for the mentally ill. She founded hospitals to separate mental patients from criminals. The patients were **treated** with kindness.

______ **6.** In this paragraph, the word **treated** means

A. amazed **C.** decided
B. stared **D.** handled

The Great Wall of China is thousands of miles long. It is three stories high. The top is wide enough for troops and horses. The wall was built by China's leaders long ago. They wanted to protect themselves from **invaders**.

______ **7.** In this paragraph, the word **invaders** means

A. attackers **C.** messengers
B. passengers **D.** friends

William Lance invented a self-waiting table. The counter where people ate remained **fixed** in one place. Five serving shelves rolled by on a track. People would take the food they wanted as it went by.

______ **8.** In this paragraph, the word **fixed** means

A. helpless **C.** motionless
B. useless **D.** tasteless

Dr. Jane C. Wright, an African American, studied medicine. She became the **director** of a cancer research center. The center was run by a college. Later, Jane served as associate dean for the college.

_____ **1.** In this paragraph, the word **director** means
A. teacher **C.** coach
B. reporter **D.** manager

The zebra belongs to the horse family. It has black and white stripes. The zebra spends time **grazing** on the African plains. Then it goes to watering holes. The lion is its enemy. The zebra bites and kicks to protect itself.

_____ **2.** In this paragraph, the word **grazing** means
A. drifting in air **C.** walking by mountains
B. feeding on grasses **D.** swimming in streams

Grains of sand drift in the wind. The sand collects, and it forms a **mound**. This is called a dune. As the winds blow, the dune will grow and change. If plants take hold, the dune will stop changing.

_____ **3.** In this paragraph, the word **mound** means
A. hill **C.** vegetable
B. desert **D.** tunnel

The yak, a member of the cattle family, lives in Tibet. It has long, thick hair for the cold climate. The yak is used for hauling heavy **bundles**. Its meat, hair, and hides are also useful.

_____ **4.** In this paragraph, the word **bundles** means
A. coats **C.** packs
B. dishes **D.** brownies

SCORE

A time **capsule** is one way to save things for people in the future to study. Objects are chosen that show what life is like. These objects are placed inside the capsule. The capsule is sealed. Then it is buried or put in a special room. Someday it will be opened.

______ **5.** In this paragraph, the word **capsule** means

A. medicine **C.** line
B. container **D.** strap

It once took ships a long time to go from the Atlantic Ocean to the Pacific Ocean. They had to go around South America. Then the Panama Canal was built. The canal shortened the **route**.

______ **6.** In this paragraph, the word **route** means

A. ticket **C.** passage
B. student **D.** nation

Fort Knox is located in Kentucky. It contains the Armor Center for the United States Army. Fort Knox is where the Treasury Department **deposits** its billions of dollars worth of gold.

______ **7.** In this paragraph, the word **deposits** means

A. favors **C.** washes
B. harms **D.** places

Dreaming is an important part of sleep. Dreams occur during a period of rapid eye movement. The eyes move quickly during this stage of sleep. If awakened during this period, a person can clearly **recall** the dream.

______ **8.** In this paragraph, the word **recall** means

A. remember **C.** forget
B. cure **D.** escape

Fog is really a low-lying cloud. It is formed near the ground or on the surface of a body of water. Fog appears because a sudden **chill** has condensed the moisture in the air.

_____ **1.** In this paragraph, the word **chill** means

A. storm
B. fever
C. warm front
D. temperature drop

The Maya once built great cities. They lived in an area that stretched from southern Mexico to Central America. Then the Maya began to **evacuate** the large cities. They moved to farms or small towns. The reason they left the cities is still unknown.

_____ **2.** In this paragraph, the word **evacuate** means

A. sweep
B. build
C. join
D. leave

Jane Goodall went to Africa to observe animals. She studied chimpanzees for a long time. Jane **realized** many things about their daily lives.

_____ **3.** In this paragraph, the word **realized** means

A. captured
B. learned
C. prepared
D. satisfied

Tasmania is an island. It is the smallest state of Australia. The land is green and has **rugged** features. Some people come from the mainland to see the natural beauty of the island.

_____ **4.** In this paragraph, the word **rugged** means

A. uneven
B. level
C. hopeless
D. careless

SCORE

Some mushrooms are good to eat. But others are **toxic**. Often an expert is the only one who can tell them apart. You can stay safe by buying your mushrooms from a store.

______ **5.** In this paragraph, the word **toxic** means

A. fruit **C.** delicious
B. crisp **D.** poisonous

A tornado is a very **fierce** storm. This funnel-shaped cloud does not last long. But it sucks up everything in its path. The strong winds can be very destructive.

______ **6.** In this paragraph, the word **fierce** means

A. friendly **C.** dangerous
B. sticky **D.** small

The stonefish lives in the ocean waters of Australia. It is well **camouflaged** because it looks like a stone. If a stonefish is stepped on, the poison from its spines can cause death.

______ **7.** In this paragraph, the word **camouflaged** means

A. detailed **C.** appeared
B. hidden **D.** exercised

Mark Wellman wanted to climb El Capitán cliff in California. He has a physical disability. He knew climbing this rock wall wouldn't be easy. He pulled himself up most of the way. Then a friend carried him to the **summit**. Mark had found a way up.

______ **8.** In this paragraph, the word **summit** means

A. peak **C.** side
B. quarrel **D.** bottom

The wolf is a large member of the dog family. It is a good hunter. Hoofed animals are its **normal** prey. The wolf inhabits areas that have few people.

______ **1.** In this paragraph, the word **normal** means

A. curious **C.** usual
B. delicious **D.** unusual

When you look at the moon, you might **detect** that you always see the same side. This is because Earth's gravity makes the moon spin very slowly. The moon will spin only one time as it makes its entire orbit around Earth.

______ **2.** In this paragraph, the word **detect** means

A. notice **C.** celebrate
B. show **D.** adjust

The shingleback lizard lives in Australia. It uses its fat tail for protection. Birds are **deceived** into thinking that the tail is the lizard's head. They attack the wrong end.

______ **3.** In this paragraph, the word **deceived** means

A. tricked **C.** thrown
B. taught **D.** floated

Luxembourg is located in Europe. It is one of the oldest and smallest **independent** countries there. This country is a leader in industry. But it maintains its dense forests and rolling hills.

______ **4.** In this paragraph, the word **independent** means

A. smart **C.** alone
B. gentle **D.** self-governing

SCORE

A starfish is a creature that lives in the ocean. It has a **minimum** of five arms. If a starfish injures or breaks off an arm, a new one will grow in its place.

______ **5.** In this paragraph, the word **minimum** means

A. best
B. at least
C. highest
D. in short

A flight simulator looks like a video game. It is a very accurate machine. It can train pilots to **react** to emergencies on an airplane. But there is no danger while they are learning.

______ **6.** In this paragraph, the word **react** means

A. murmur
B. destroy
C. respond
D. satisfy

Long ago doctors began to suspect that the two sides of the brain work differently. Today some people think that the left side **controls** how we solve problems. They believe the right side guides how we feel about things.

______ **7.** In this paragraph, the word **controls** means

A. jumps
B. charges
C. promises
D. directs

Golda Meir worked hard to create the state of Israel. It is a homeland for the Jewish people. Golda **served** as prime minister of Israel for five years. She helped make Israel strong.

______ **8.** In this paragraph, the word **served** means

A. walked away
B. put into play
C. performed the duties of
D. gave food and drink to

Read each paragraph. Write a word that makes sense on each line.

Since David loved sports so much, he joined a **(1)** ____________ team. He practiced every day to improve his **(2)** ____________.

The principal asked our class to paint the **(3)** ____________ behind the school. We decided to paint a scene showing trees and colorful **(4)** ____________.

Karla's family is going on vacation. They are planning to travel by **(5)** ____________. I'm going to feed their **(6)** ____________ while they are away.

To check your answers, turn to page 60.

Read each paragraph. Write a sentence that makes sense on each line.

Ashley thought hard. What could she invent for the contest? **(1)** ______________________________

______________________________________.

She knew that an invention should solve a problem. Then Ashley saw her little brother playing outside. He was having trouble. **(2)** ______________________________

______________________________________.

Now she knew what to invent! **(3)** ______________________________

______________________________________.

Marcus was hiking in the forest. Suddenly he heard a noise in the trees. What could it be?

(4) ______________________________________.

Marcus looked up and saw something strange.

(5) ______________________________________.

He quickly aimed his camera and took a picture. How surprised he was when his film was developed!

(6) ______________________________________.

To check your answers, turn to page 60.

Check Yourself

Working with Context, Page 4

2. A **3.** B

To check your answers to pages 6–29, see page 61.

Writing, Page 30

Possible answers include:

1. umbrella or raincoat
2. head or clothes
3. drum or tuba
4. play or march
5. nails or wood
6. strange or wonderful

Writing, Page 31

Possible answers include:

1. She dug deeper. She ran for help.
2. It was a bag of coins. It was a ring she had lost.
3. She would look for the owner. She would put it in a safe place.
4. She could walk dogs. She could be a pet-sitter.
5. She was going on vacation. She needed help with her yard.
6. She will water Ms. Fielder's plants. She will mow Ms. Fielder's yard.

To check your answers to pages 32–57, see page 62.

Writing, Page 58

Possible answers include:

1. soccer or baseball
2. kicking or throwing
3. wall or fence
4. birds or flowers
5. car or airplane
6. pets or fish

Writing, Page 59

Possible answers include:

1. She could invent a better lunch box. She could invent a game.
2. His kite string was tangled. His shoelace kept coming untied.
3. She'd make a string holder. She would make a shoelace clip.
4. It might be a huge bird. It might be a monkey.
5. The tree was full of bats. A squirrel was flying.
6. The picture showed only leaves. The picture was too blurry.

Check Yourself

	Unit 1 pp. 6–7	Unit 2 pp. 8–9	Unit 3 pp. 10–11	Unit 4 pp. 12–13	Unit 5 pp. 14–15	Unit 6 pp. 16–17	Unit 7 pp. 18–19	Unit 8 pp. 20–21	Unit 9 pp. 22–23	Unit 10 pp. 24–25	Unit 11 pp. 26–27	Unit 12 pp. 28–29
1.	B	C	B	D	B	D	B	C	A	B	C	A
2.	A	B	A	A	A	C	C	D	D	D	D	C
3.	C	A	A	C	C	D	D	B	B	C	D	D
4.	B	D	D	C	D	C	B	A	D	A	B	B
5.	D	A	B	A	C	B	A	C	C	A	D	C
6.	C	B	C	B	C	C	D	C	A	C	A	A
7.	A	D	B	B	D	A	C	B	B	B	A	D
8.	B	C	D	D	B	B	C	A	C	D	C	B
9.	D	B	D	A	A	B	A	D	A	D	B	A
10.	C	A	B	B	D	A	B	D	B	B	A	B
11.	B	B	B	B	C	A	B	B	C	C	A	D
12.	A	A	A	C	B	C	A	A	B	A	C	A
13.	A	D	C	D	B	C	C	C	D	A	D	C
14.	C	B	D	C	A	D	D	B	B	B	C	B
15.	B	C	A	A	B	D	D	C	C	D	B	D
16.	D	D	B	D	C	B	C	A	A	C	D	C

Unit 13 pp. 32–33	Unit 14 pp. 34–35	Unit 15 pp. 36–37	Unit 16 pp. 38–39	Unit 17 pp. 40–41	Unit 18 pp. 42–43	Unit 19 pp. 44–45	Unit 20 pp. 46–47	Unit 21 pp. 48–49	Unit 22 pp. 50–51	Unit 23 pp. 52–53	Unit 24 pp. 54–55	Unit 25 pp. 56–57
1. B	**1.** B	**1.** C	**1.** C	**1.** C	**1.** C	**1.** C	**1.** D	**1.** A	**1.** C	**1.** D	**1.** D	**1.** C
2. A	**2.** C	**2.** A	**2.** D	**2.** B	**2.** D	**2.** A	**2.** C	**2.** D	**2.** B	**2.** B	**2.** D	**2.** A
3. B	**3.** D	**3.** B	**3.** A	**3.** C	**3.** D	**3.** B	**3.** D	**3.** B	**3.** A	**3.** A	**3.** B	**3.** A
4. D	**4.** A	**4.** A	**4.** C	**4.** A	**4.** B	**4.** D	**4.** B	**4.** A	**4.** B	**4.** C	**4.** A	**4.** D
5. C	**5.** A	**5.** C	**5.** B	**5.** D	**5.** D	**5.** A	**5.** A	**5.** C	**5.** B	**5.** B	**5.** D	**5.** B
6. B	**6.** B	**6.** D	**6.** D	**6.** C	**6.** B	**6.** D	**6.** B	**6.** A	**6.** D	**6.** C	**6.** C	**6.** C
7. A	**7.** B	**7.** D	**7.** A	**7.** B	**7.** A	**7.** C	**7.** D	**7.** D	**7.** A	**7.** D	**7.** B	**7.** D
8. B	**8.** A	**8.** A	**8.** A	**8.** B	**8.** B	**8.** B	**8.** C	**8.** D	**8.** C	**8.** A	**8.** A	**8.** C